Challenges and Prospects of Urban Productive Safety Net Programe

Challenges and Prospects of Urban Productive Safety Net Programe

Dr. Karanam Viswa Bhushan

GenNext Publication

First Published, 2021

Published by

GenNext Publication
5, Ansari Road
Daryaganj, New Delhi-110002
Phone: 9811692060
E-mail: gennextpublication@hotmail.com

Printed at: Gyan Press, Delhi.

Cataloging in Publication Data—DK
Courtesy: D.K. Agencies (P) Ltd. <docinfo@dkagencies.com>

Bhushan, Karanam Viswa, 1963- **author.**
Challenges and prospects of urban productive safety net programme / Dr. Karanam Viswa Bhushan.
pages cm
Includes bibliographical references.
ISBN 9789353243289 (HB)
"An Imprint of Kalpaz Publication"

1. Food security—Ethiopia—Addis Ababa. 2. Food security—Government policy—Ethiopia—Addis Ababa. 3. Rural development projects—Ethiopia—Addis Ababa. 4. Addis Ababa (Ethiopia)—Rural conditions. I. Title.

LCC HD9017.E83A33 2021 | DDC 338.19633 23

Contents

Acknowledgements

First of all I thank the Almighty God for his heavenly blessings.

I would like to express my gratitude to my student Kidist Mekete for her participation and involvement during the research work.

I would like to express my heart-felt thanks and deepest gratitude to all those who encouraged to the book publication.

I would like to thank the staff of Kirkose sub city administration food security and job creation office for providing me all relevant information for the research work.

It is great pleasure to extend my gratitude to my beloved sister Asha Jyothi and her family members for their encouragement and inspiration.

List of Tables

Chapter One

Introduction

Several countries in the world, mainly developing countries are facing many problems which are associated with the livelihood of their citizens as access to food has been a challenge. Food security has been in the public eye for a long time and it began to make a series impact on the development debate in 1970s. Nevertheless, such countries are still on their long lasting strives to solve such interwoven problems. And to improve the livelihood of society to bring about changes in terms of social, economic, environmental, institutional, and infrastructural and the like though they encounter various ups and downs against their efforts as most of them are in developing world, resource poor, and dependent on external aid and transfer (Max well, 2001).

Food insecurity is the lack of access to sufficient food. It occurs as chronic or transitory. Chronic food insecurity is a continuous inadequacy of diets whereas transitory food insecurity is temporal decline in a household's access to enough food (Reutlinger, 1998).

This food insecurity is resulting from recumbent drought; low input and output of subsistence agriculture, widespread poverty and environmental degradation are some of major challenges facing developing countries, especially in Africa, South of the Sahara. This is emanated from population pressure and fan fragmentation (Agrekon, 2009). Developing and least developed countries use policies and programs to improve the dire situation of food insecurity by creating employment and accessing job opportunities; and implementing urban safety net programs for the poor.

1.1 Background of the Study

Cities Of Food Security And Developmental Safety Net Urban food security means that every citizen will have a steady, unbroken diet that will bring about 2200 calories to daily consumption, making it healthy and productive. Developmental Safety Nets (NFTP) is linked to individuals and families with severe food insecurity in their food production and sustainable livelihoods, with a view to expanding their income generating options and increasing productivity to ensure their Food security and sustainably guarantee their food security. While food security is an unprecedented phenomenon in every part of the world, the problem is widespread in developing countries. The expansion of this problem is likely to have negative effects on economic, social, political, cultural and environmental factors of the 870 million people in the world, about 870 million are inadequate, with one in eight men suffering from this problem. The majority of the affected people live in developing countries, especially in the sub-Saharan Africa. The world's most notable examples of food insecurity in urban areas are the dependence on the daily trading system, the lack of attention to agriculture and natural resources, the inadequate livelihoods of non-recurring livelihoods, the lack of legal boundaries with landholding, the insufficient supply of safe drinking water, Lack of access to adequate sanitation and health facilities, and weak social interconnection networks and others. In addition, various studies indicate that citizens living under the poverty line are most likely to be affected by the economic insecurity resulting in the absence of governmental support for citizens who are living illegally and disinterested and living in poverty reduction schemes. According to the World Food Program information, over one million people are at risk of being over-recognized because of the world food inflation since 2008, and that 75% of these are urban dwellers. (Food Security Strategy [FSS], 2007)

According to the Central Statistical Agency, (2015) urban population is estimated to reach 18.7 million, an increase of 5.2 percent annually, which is expected to increase in the future. The urban population will rise to a great extent, with varying complexity and complexity, according to urban development. The problem of food insecurity in our country is largely due to the lack of labor force, poor marketing chains, and lack of developmental administration, diet, culture, employment, and cultural well-being.

The Government of Ethiopia (GoE) developed the Urban Food Security Strategy (UFSS) in 2015. This was followed by a 10-year Urban Job Creation and Food Security Program (UJCFSP). The objective of the UJCFSP is to alleviate urban food insecurity and tackle the increasing levels of vulnerability by supporting over 4.7 million urban poor living in 972 cities and towns. This is expected to be achieved over a long-term period through a gradual roll-out plan indifferent phases starting with big cities that have a population of over 100,000 people.

The Urban Productive Safety Net Program, the first of its kind in urban areas, is a five-year phase of the Government program targeting 11 major cities. According to a survey conducted by the Central Statistical Agency (CSA) of 2015, the population of Addis Ababa is 4 million. The population growth rate is 2.1% annually and the total an increment of

5.2 percent annually. The population growth in cities has increased steadily, with the growth trajectory of food insecure Lag is inevitable in view of the strong negative impact. It is also estimated that 18.9 percent of the poverty rate in Addis Ababa (CSA, 2015). According to World Bank report (2015) Addis Ababa city accounts 470,000 people under poverty line (World Bank, 2015).

The Survey conducted by the Central Statistics Agency indicated that 18.9 percent of the population in Addis Ababa is living below the general poverty line or unable to buy basic food and non-food items. In general, the food security problem in our country is generally underrepresented, the lack of labors, the weak marketing chain, the lack of developmental administration, the food security problem has become a great international agenda, and many countries are addressing the realities of the crisis in various national social services and food security programs.

1.2. Description of the Study Area

Addis Ababa lies at an elevation of 2,300m (7,500 ft) and is a grassland biome, located at 9°12483N 38°442243E Coordinates: 9°12483N 38°442243E.[17] The city lies at the foot of Mount Entoto and forms part of the watershed for the Awash. From its lowest point, around Bole International Airport, at 2,326m (7,631 ft) above sea level in the southern periphery, the city rises to over 3,000m (9,800 ft) in the Entoto Mountains to the north.

Addis Ababa is the largest as well as the dominant political, economic cultural and historical city of the country established as a center base of "FIL WUHA" during Minilik II 1887. It has both a city and state. It is where the African Union and its predecessor, the OAU are based. It also hosts headquarter of the United Nations Economic Commission for Africa (UNECA) and numerous other continental and international organizations.

Kirkos sub city one the oldest sub city from 10 sub city. It has administrative boundary and the total area 14.65 km^2 within 11 woreda 57 sub-woreda and 474 blocks. The geographical location of the sub city is situated in the central part of Addis Ababa, bounded from south by Nifas silk lafto & Bole From west Lideta, from east Bole, from north Arada & Yeka.

The sub-city was established by the proclamation No. 1/1995 in the aim of ensuring good governance, peace and democracy, social and economic problems.

1.3. Statement of the Problem

Ethiopia experiences quite high poverty rate in urban areas, particularly in large cities; the urban-rural poverty rate differential is low in comparison to other countries. The total national poverty head count in 2011 was 29.6 percent (30.4 percent in rural Ethiopia and 25.7 percent in urban areas). Poverty rates in Addis Ababa and Dire Dawa were as high as 28.1 percent and 28.3 percent, respectively. The poverty gap index is estimated to be 8 percent in rural Ethiopia and 6.9 percent in urban Ethiopia. In large cities, poverty has been falling, but not as fast as in rural areas and smaller urban centers. From 2005 to 2011, consumption growth was negative for the poorest 15 percent of the urban population and for the majority of households in Addis Ababa as wages did not increase to compensate households for the rising food prices that they faced. One-fifth of Ethiopia's urban population lives in Addis Ababa and reducing poverty rates in this and other large urban centers is a key priority toward addressing poverty reduction in Ethiopia in general. (Urban Productive Safety Net Program Implementation Manual)

The problem of food insecurity in urban settings is chronic and complex in areas congested and inner part of the city of Addis Ababa when we compare from peripheral part of the city. Kirkos sub city located at the most inner part of the city, accommodates large number of slum residents than those sub cities which have expansion areas like Bole and Yeka.

The situational analysis of the urban food Security Strategy is not effective as we compared from the rural part of Ethiopia. This is due to high number of rural urban migration for job opportunities and better livelihood. As the capital of the country, Addis Ababa serves as a center of attraction from the whole part of the country to get job opportunities. Particularly, inner part of the city like Kirkos sub city hosts greater proportion of urban poor. Hence, the central parts of the city face huge challenges of food insecurity. (Urban Productive Safety Net Program Implementation Manual)

The following are the most pressing issues and causes of food insecurity in kirkos sub city; unsystematic rural-urban migration, lack of adequate employment opportunities; lack of integration among take holders of social protection for disadvantaged groups; underutilized potential of urban agriculture; lack of modern market exchange system; lack of efficient service delivery; lack of conducive working environment; gap between job seeker and attitudinal difference. The problems associated with the process of identifying the right target groups i.e. the most vulnerable groups in the sub city is another challenge. The city government of Addis Ababa has put in place a number of food security safety net programs. However, due to the abovementioned problems, a significant number of people in urban areas are unemployed and as a result, they are facing food insecurity and living in difficult circumstances.

Moreover, the number of street dwellers, beggars, people with mental disorder, juvenile delinquency, disadvantaged groups and other victims of social problems and ills are increasing from time to time. There are initiatives to ensure employment opportunities, rehabilitating, reintegrating and reunifying the victims of social challenges and problems. This study is therefore, focuses on assessing the challenges and prospects of urban safety net program in Addis Ababa City Administration particularly in kirkos sub city.

1.4 Research Question

The study aims at answering the following research questions

1. What are the prospects of urban safety net program in kirkos sub city?
2. What are the major challenges of urban safety net program in kirkos sub city?
3. What is the Targeting procedure in kirkos sub city?

1.5 Objectives of the Study

1.5.1 General Objective

The general objective of the study is to assess the challenges and prospects of urban safety net program in Addis Ababa City Administration kirkos sub city.

1.5.2 Specific Objective

In order to achieve the general objective, the following specific objectives are developed.

- To identify the prospects of urban safety net program in kirkos sub city
- To assess the major challenges of urban safety net program in kirkos sub city
- To explore the Targeting Process in Kirkose sub city

1.6 Scope of the Study

The scope of the study thematically covers the beneficial of the selected woredas in Addis Ababa in Kirkos sub-city, the challenge and the prospects of urban safety net program.

1.6.1 Spatial Scope

The spatial scope of the study had restricted to the Kirkos sub-city of Addis Ababa in which the beneficiaries are found.

1.6.2 Temporal scope

The time of this study covers from the proposal preparation to the finalization of the whole works scope.

1.7. Significance of the Study

The study outcomes will have two major values in terms of contribution of knowledge and benefits the concerned communities of the Sub city resident. It is hoped that this research will add to the limited knowledge available in the study area regarding the economic, social and environmental contribution because they participate on public works like greenery and solid waste management. The outcome of the study may also be used for policy considerations, for planning and designing job opportunities to vulnerable groups.

The study also identifies the prospect and challenges the sub city safety net program in the study area and creates awareness for the residents about the multifunctional values of safety net program in the study beneficial woredas.

Moreover, the study will be helpful for other researcher as a way in to do further research on the issue at hand. On the second position the benefits of the findings of the study will be to satisfy society in terms of environmental, social and economic terms. Finally, the study will be important source of information for urban safety net program job opportunity plan, input for further study and academics working on urban safety net program implementation as well as for societal satisfaction.

1.8 Limitation of the study

This study may face limitations intermesh of unwillingness of the respondents in the study area to fill the questionnaire and return back. This may challenges the research process that may ultimately the quality of the study. On the other hand lack of organized data and important related documents may also encounter the study. However, with possible maximum efforts of the researcher the problem was tackled by motivating participants to reveal relevant and realistic information or data.

1.9 Organization of the Paper

The thesis is organized into five chapters. Following this introduction part of the study, the remaining chapters are organized as follows. The second chapter presents review of relevant literature. The third chapter deals with the research methodology. The fourth chapter presents results and discussion. Finally, the fifth chapter presents the conclusion and recommendations of the study.

Chapter Two

Literature Review

2.1 Introduction

Literature review is a survey of scholarly sources that provides an overview of a particular topic. It generally follows a discussion of the paper's thesis statement or the study's goals or purpose. (Decristofaro, and Collins, 2010).

This chapter presents review of related literature on Urban Productive safety net Program. The review particularly focuses on topics that are related to the thematic concepts that constitute the framework of the study, whereas the framework was designed in such a way, that it can describe the objectives of the study. This review of literature emphasizes on concepts, ideas, and findings that are related to the objectives of the study. The review of the related literature is presented concepts and definition of related idea.

2.2 Concepts and definitions of food Security and Safety net Program

2.2.1 Definition of food Security Program

The concept of food security originated as part of the discussion on international food problems at the world food conference of 1974. Conceptually, it has gone through several stages but now a days it is mostly defined as access by all people at all times to sufficient food for active and healthy life' (World Bank, 1986).

The definition encompasses three main dimensions of food security namely availability, adequacy and accessibility of food. Food availability refers to sufficiency food production and involves the concept of food sufficiency to sustain life for the entire population. It also implies that food and its achievements can be targeted at global, regional, national, sub-national household or individual level; the latter two, however, have increasingly become the main focus of studies now a day (Dagnew, 1994).

Though food security interpreted in many ways may be defined here as "access by all people at all time to enough food for active and health life" (Reutlinger, 1998). More specifically, the household's food security refers to the "ability of household members to assure them sustained access to sufficient quantity of food to live active and healthy life" (Dagnew, 1994).

Based on the intensive empirical investigation on subsistence farmers in Ethiopia, Getachew (1995) has come out with contextual definition of food security as a household's ability to establish access to productive resources such as land, livestock, agricultural inputs and family labor combined to produce food or cash. In line of this Reutlinger identified five essential components should be taken into account for the better understating of food security situations; these are food availability, access to food, sustainability, food entitlement and vulnerability (Reutlinger, 1998).

Production and supply are dependable in the face of possible production shortage due to general causes, such as natural disasters and civil disturbances (Lal, etai, 2002). Food accessibility encompasses not only transportation and marketing but also the means by which food is acquired.

Producing an adequate food is not enough; consumers must be in a position to purchase or obtain the necessary food (Lat, et ai, 2002). The problem of food security affects nations and citizens in a way that it increases people's vulnerability to disease, curtails learning capability, reduces productivity, and ultimately makes it difficult for citizens and nations to extricate themselves from the cycle of poverty (Routlinger, 1998). In response to this serious problem the countries that suffer from the problem adopt various policy strategies to achieve the food security of their citizens.

2.2.2 Definitions Safety net program

Safety net is a concept defined based on its purpose, components, target beneficiaries and Ownership of the programs. Accordingly, different literatures define safety nets having economic, social, cultural and political back ground of countries at stake. Authors like Devereux and Wheeler (2004) define safety nets as interventions that protect lives and ensure a minimum subsistence in times of crisis, and typically food based and short term in nature. Raised on what they constitute, safety nets are programs that include a broad range of mechanisms that protect individuals or households against poverty. This can be through individuals and/or household risk sharing, social services, social insurance programs, publicly funded transfers and income generation programs (Girma and Holden).

Alternative views of safety nets are, for example, those of WFP (2012), where their role is seen in a broader social context to not only increase consumption per capital but also to have a distributive function and create political stability. Accordingly, safety nets are defined as public interventions, which are designed to play a distributive role of resource transferring towards the poorer members of society to bring them out of poverty and provide greater opportunity for individuals to mitigate risks from unforeseen contingencies. On the other hand, Holzmallli and Jorgensen (1999) argue that public interventions as a safety net assist in better managing income risks, as well as contributing to social cohesion.

Safety nets therefore do not only protect individuals from transient periods of poverty, say due to loss of employment, sudden illness, or natural disasters, but also serve to protect individuals from lifetime poverty that can arise from, say, lack of education and poor health, particularly in childhood (MORDA, 2006).

2.2.3 Urban Productive Safety Net Program (UPSNP)

2.3.1 Background and Context

The Government of Ethiopia (GOE) has completed the first Growth and Transformation Plan (GTP I) (2010/11–2014/15), which set a long-term goal for Ethiopia to become a lower middle-income country by 2025. The growth rate of at least 11.2 percent per year was set and achieved during the plan period. The second phase of the GTP (GTP II 2016-2020) is essentially a continuation of GTP I objectives and priorities are given to key sectors such as industry and agriculture as drivers of sustained economic growth and job creation. The GTP II also reaffirms the GOE's commitment to human development. The programs of development partners (DPs) are broadly aligned with the GTP II priorities.

There is strong record of reducing extreme poverty in recent years. The main drivers of this progress have been rural based namely, agricultural growth, provision of basic services, and rural safety nets. However, the structural transformation that is needed in value addition (a shift from low value/wage to high value/wage sectors) has been in adequate to make significant contribution to poverty reduction.

Although Ethiopia remains predominantly rural, urbanization is taking place, and as Ethiopia urbanizes, poverty becomes more urban. In 2000, 11 percent of Ethiopia's poor lived in cities, but this rose to 14 percent in 2011. The urban population reached 11.9 million by the last census in 2007 and was estimated to reach 16.7 million in 2014, with an average population growth rate of 3.8 percent. Urban population is projected to triple by 2034 reaching 30 percent of the total population. World Bank 2015, Ethiopia Urbanization Review as more of the urban poor live in large urban centers, expanding development programs to address key challenges to urban poverty reduction is imperative.

An economically dynamic urban transformation is necessary for Ethiopia to reach middle-income status, end poverty, and improve shared prosperity. Getting urban growth correct now is crucial to developing the type of cities that foster inclusive growth in the long run. If managed proactively, urban population growth presents an opportunity to shift the structure and location of economic activity from rural agriculture to the larger and more diversified urban industrial and service sectors. If not managed proactively, rapid urban population growth may pose a demographic challenge as cities struggle to provide citizens with jobs, infrastructure and services, and housing. World Bank 2015, Ethiopia Urbanization Review.

Although urban poverty rates in Ethiopia are quite high, particularly in the large cities, the urban-rural poverty rate differential is low in comparison to other countries. The total national poverty head count in 2011 was 29.6 percent (30.4 percent in rural Ethiopia and 25.7 percent in urban areas). Poverty rates in Addis Ababa and Dire Dawa were as high as 28.1 percent and 28.3 percent, respectively. The poverty gap index is estimated to be 8 percent in rural Ethiopia and 6.9 percent in urban Ethiopia. In large cities, poverty has been falling, but not as fast as in rural areas and smaller urban centers. From 2005 to 2011, consumption growth was negative for the poorest 15 percent of the urban population and for the majority of households in Addis Ababa as wages did not increase to compensate households for the rising food prices that they faced. One-fifth of Ethiopia's urban population lives in Addis Ababa and reducing poverty rates in this and other large urban centers is a key priority toward addressing poverty reduction in Ethiopia in general.

The problem of food insecurity in urban settings is chronic and complex. Moreover, the marketing system for agriculture products is not well developed to promote the growth of industrialization; boost employment opportunities and linkage with the rural areas is improving but still at an infant sage due to the slowly expanding infrastructure and services. Unless urban centers become centers of modern market exchange, technology transfer, and good governance, they may negatively affect and slow down the overall development of the country. In order to improve this situation in urban areas, the government of Ethiopia has designed urban food security strategy and job creation and food security program. Urban Productive Safety Net Program (UPSNP manual, 2016 p. 2)

The situational analysis of the Urban food Security Strategy (UPSNP manual, 2016 p. 2), has established that some of the root causes of food insecurity in urban areas are: unsystematic rural-urban migration (that is urban rural migration not guided by economic indicators); lack of adequate employment opportunities; lack of integrated social protection for disadvantaged groups; underutilized potential of urban agriculture; lack of modern market exchange system; lack of efficient service delivery; lack of conducive working environment; poor solid and liquid waste management; and environmental, natural and man-made hazards. Urban areas are also severely affected by price hikes that arise from production falls due to drought and other natural disasters.

Due to aforementioned problems, a significant number of people in urban areas are unemployed and underemployed and as a result, they are facing food insecurity and living in difficult circumstances. Moreover, the number of street dwellers, beggars, people with mental disorder, juvenile delinquency, disadvantaged groups and other victims of social problems and evils are increasing from time to time. Urban Productive Safety Net Program (UPSNP manual, 2016 p. 2).

> The Government is committed to minimizing the chronic problems of the urban dwellers thereby improving their quality of life by strengthening rehabilitative and preventive measures in line with the GTP II and the Sustainable Development Goals (SDGs). There are initiatives to ensure employment opportunities, rehabilitating, reintegrating and reunifying the victims of social evils and problems. Urban Productive Safety Net Program (UPSNP manual, 2016 p. 2).

The Ministry of Urban Development and Housing (MOUDH), as key Government executive organ, is given the mandate to block the urban food insecurity and poverty. To this end, the ministry has developed Urban Job Creation and Food Security Strategy and Program as part of the National Social Protection Policy and Strategy of the country. The initial phase of the program is implemented in collaboration with various stakeholders and the World Bank as development partners financing the program. Urban Productive Safety Net Program (UPSNP) manual, 2016 p.2

The rural PSNP, which has been implemented since 2005, has demonstrated that safety nets are important tools for addressing chronic food insecurity. Based on these experiences, the MOUDH has led the design of a systematic productive urban safety net and livelihood support intervention which will be implemented through a 10-year program framework. The long-term program framework has an objective of reaching 4.7 million poor in 972 urban areas by implementing productive and predictable urban safety nets and complimentary livelihood interventions. The first phase supported by the UPSNP runs from 2016/17 to 2020/21 in 11 cities (Addis Ababa, Adama, Dessie, Mekele, Hawassa, Dire Dawa, Harari, Gambella, Asosa, Jigjiga and Asayita) and will focus on putting in place basic safety net building blocks, including productive and predictable transfers through public work (PW), livelihood interventions and capacity building. Urban Productive Safety Net Program (UPSNP) manual, 2016 p. 3)

2.2.3 Targeting Process

Through a combination of geographic targeting, community-based targeting, proxy means tests and self-selection. A geographically targeted program in that it operates only in selected cities/towns in Ethiopia. The cities included in the program are cities with the highest rates of poverty. Although the program will scale to cover all areas of the city, in the first year it will target beneficiaries in the poorer parts of the city based on poverty maps and expand to other parts of the city in the second and third year. The process of targeting is *bottom up* starting from ketena! kebele! woreda/sub-city ! city level where beneficiary numbers are aggregated city poverty maps have produced three level of poverty – low (< 20%), moderate (between 20% and 40%) and high (> 40%). In the first year of implementation, the program will start in a selection of the poorest woredas (those with high and moderate poverty rates) with the remaining high and moderate poverty woredas being included in the second year. In the final year, low poverty woredas will also be included.

The specific steps for area/beneficiary targeting are as follows:

Step 1: Community/Ketena Targeting Committee or Community/Ketena Care Coalitions are established (or strengthened where they exist) in each community composed of 7, 9 or 11 members for ease of decision making of which 3-4 members will be women. The distribution is as follows:

- Two community elders (one woman and one man)
- One NGO representative with experience in supporting vulnerable groups in urban areas
- One representative of community based institutions (e.g., Idir/Clan Leader)
- Two representatives of professions (e.g., teachers, health)
- 2-3 representatives of associations (e.g. disability association, elder association, women and youth) depending on availability and
- One social worker

Step 2: The poorest woredas/kebeles are selected for the first year of implementation using 2011 within-city poverty maps.

Step 3: Ketena Targeting Committees rank and select beneficiaries. The list is made public.

Step 4: Kebele/woreda personnel and social workers oversee the community targeting process in the kebele/woreda.

Step 5: Lists of registered HHs and members are updated to take into account any recent changes, and an additional list of unregistered members or HHs is developed containing those that have been residing in the woreda/ kebele for at least six months.

Step 6: UPSNP PCU at sub-City level provides technical support to woreda/kebele/ketena targeting committees.

Step 7: The woreda office provides information to an independent data collection agency contracted by the program who works with UPSNP staff to sample HHs.

Step 8: HHs for whom the assignment to beneficiary or non-beneficiary is queried are discussed by woreda officials, program staff, and the Ketena Targeting Committee and a final decision is made. The final list of proposed beneficiaries is made public.

Step 9: For all eligible HHs, categorical targeting will be used to determine who is eligible for conditional and unconditional transfers.

Step 10: Those eligible for permanent unconditional transfers who would like to receive these transfers register and provide verification of age (above 65 years only) or of their disability or chronic illness that prevents them from being able to perform a co-responsibility for the transfer.

Step 11: HHs eligible for temporary unconditional transfers are identified by the social worker and presented to Ketena Targeting Committee for consideration.

Step 12: This list will not include street dwellers that will be targeted separately by skilled professionals that are experienced in tracking and identifying these individuals.

Step 13: A Woreda Appeals Committee allows targeting decisions to be appealed

2.4.5 Prospect of Urban Safety Net Program in Ethiopia

The objective of the Urban Productive Safety net Program is to Support the Government of Ethiopia to Improve income of targeted poor households and establish urban safety net mechanisms There are Three components to the program, the first component begin safety net support. This component will support the delivery of a predictable, timely, and productive safety net through conditional and unconditional safety net transfers. The program will ensure that various safety net principles such as primacy, adequacy, and predictability of transfer are respected. The second component is the livelihood services. This component will support interventions that will facilitate graduation from the program and promote moving out of poverty. The target groups for these interventions are individual in households receiving conditional Transfers who desire more and higher - paid work. One individual per household receive this support which will result in a total of individuals eligible for this component. The individual will be selected by the household. The support will be implemented by the stop center directorate in the urban food security and Job Creation Agency. We established one stop Centers in woredas/kebeles. Some of the functions will strengthen of project systems for targeting, monitoring and evaluation and MIS payments, and citizen's engagement (CE). It also finance capacity building (human resource, training, administrative, and physical capacity) and strengthening program management (coordination, financial management (FM), procurement, and safeguards. (World Bank, 2015)

2.4.6 Challenges of Urban Safety Nets

The serious gap in urban coverage is due not only to a

common preoccupation with the need for social assistance in rural areas but also by the complexities of identifying and targeting urban beneficiaries. Reaching out to targeted beneficiaries is often problematic as people might have just moved to urban areas or are living in informal settlements. To address such complexities, urban safety nets need to be designed to match the unique characteristics of specific urban contexts, rather than simply replicate those implemented in rural areas. Social safety net program adapted to urban contexts are beginning to emerge, although more practical learning, experimentation and knowledge exchange are needed. (World Bank, 2015)

2.3 Cross country Experience

Under this section, experience of developing counties in relation with labor based safety net is reviewed. Some major implementation issues of public works in India, some Latin American countries and Africa are described. The major implementation issues related to safety nets are the mechanisms of beneficiary selection, financing and flow of funds, project type and site selection and program monitoring and evaluation. All these aspects are influenced by the institutional capacities. Several implementation issues of safety net programs are quite diverse across countries. Indeed, the nature of safety net programs has been related to their implementation i.e. supply driven and demand driven programs are implemented differently. Looking at cross-country evidences of public works implementation is significant for the purpose of this study. Among the world's largest and best known rural and urban public works are India's Jawahar RojgarYojana (JRY) and the Employment Assurance Scheme (EAS), both designed to help ensure gainful employment for poor households and to contribute to community asset creation (infrastructure). The two programs are administered differently (Nayyar, 2002).

The administration of JRY is very complex and of the total fund made available three Fourth of it is earmarked for various rural infrastructure schemes. Each state received funds based on the proportion of poor persons residing in them. States in turn allocate JRY funds to district based on population shares and an index of backwardness. From JRY, funds pass down to block and village *level* strictly according to population share. The village elected local bodies (Panachyats), subject to the basic program guidelines and district Rural Development Authority, administrates work plans and contracts.

According to World Bank (1998), JRY generates an estimated one million person days of employment per annum. Some 30 to 40 percent potential beneficiaries were participating in the program. JRY is largely supply driven, implemented by local bodies but subject to pre- determined centrally driven guidelines.

Contrast to JR Y, EAS is demand driven in which district authorities apply directly to the central administration for funding and allocations. Unlike JRY, in the EAS the district collector has over all responsibilities for coordinating the work and allocating funds among blocks within a district (Nayyar, 2002).

In countries like Bolivia, Honduras, Elsalvador, Peru, Panama and Nicaragua, small-scale public works projects have been implemented under the aegis of Social Investment Funds (SIFs). These projects are demand driven i.e. they are submitted by the community. The communities themselves implement the projects after being proven by SIFs. The projects have focused mainly on social infrastructure and often created temporary jobs. For instance, in Bolivia, the targeting and implementation performance have been good. Seventy seven percent of the participants came from the poorest 40 percent of the population. After the intervention, the average worker improved his/her income by 67 percent (Jorgenson et al. 1992).

In Africa too, quite a few public works projects have been financed and sponsored by Social Investment Funds. By 1998, there were 19 public works projects implemented through social funds in 12 African countries, including Senegal, Guinea-Bissau, Madagascar, Mauritania, and Ghana (Frigenti and Harth, 1998).

Several donors in addition to the World Bank supported over half of these projects. The principles are the same as in Latin America, with project proposals prepared by communities and submitted to the SIFs for approval and financing. In Senegal, Agencies d'Execution des Travauxd' interet Public Contraries Sous-Emploi (AGETlP), success in implementing public works was largely due to its insulation politics (Guush, Kumarand Alemayehu 2011)

In contrast, Ghana's public works project was integrated into government ministries and consequently faced delays in implementation. Line departments of governments in some African countries have implemented public works projects on a large-scale, albeit with donor funds. In implementing such projects, however, evidence suggests that the public works departments of governments typically favored equipment-based methods because they were perceived to be superior to labor- intensive methods and completed the work faster. It is quite possible that in some countries, equipment-intensive projects may offer greater opportunities for rent seeking (World Food Program, 1996).

In some countries, such as Ghana, the task of implementing public works was entrusted to private contractors. Evidence suggests that contractors have also been reluctant to adopt labor-intensive public works, largely because of the complexities of managing large labor gangs (World Food Program, 1996).

2.4 Ethiopia's Cities Food Guarantee Status

According to the Central Statistical Agency data, urban population is estimated to reach 18.7 million, an increase of 5.2 percent annually, which is expected to increase in the future. The urban population will rise to a great extent, with varying complexity and complexity, according to urban development. The problem of food insecurity in our country is largely due to the lack of labor force, poor marketing chains, and lack of developmental administration, diet, culture, employment, and cultural well-being. The Central Statistical Agency (CSA) estimates that for 2011-11, food poverty is defined as a year for an adult in 1985, and a gross poverty line of Birr 3781 and below. Based on the study, 29.6 percent of urban dwellers in urban areas have a 25.7 percent share of the population below the general poverty line, or are able to purchase basic food and non-food items. Poverty level in the cities of Ethiopia Studies in our country over the last several years indicates that the poverty rate, especially poverty rate and the under-poverty rate, is decreasing from time to time.

According to the European Central Statistical Agency, from 1999 to 2010/11, data from showed that the poverty rate in urban areas decreased from 36.5 percent to 27.9 percent. For this reason, the government is working to reduce poverty and ensure food security. Many of the jobs that are contributing to poverty are one of the weaknesses in job creation and urban unemployment. On the other hand, some parts of the community should have a distorted view of work. In addition, our society has a well-respected tradition, but as the aid is inadequate, inadequate and inadequate, the absence of sustainability, rather than sustainability, the more awe-inspiring cause of unprotected conflict. (Food Security Strategy 2008-2017)

2.5 Food security and changes in the City of Addis Ababa

The population growth in cities has increased steadily and steadily, with the growth trajectory of food insecure Lag is inevitable in view of the strong negative impact. It is estimated that 18.9 percent of the poverty rate in Addis Ababa is lower than the poverty rate in 2015, compared with the urban population below the poverty line of 9.2 percent. The Central Statistical Agency estimates that in 1995/6000, Food poverty was estimated at 648 bc for an adult, and income from the poverty line at 1075 and below. Food security for the year 2010/2011 is estimated to be approximately $ 3781 per year and by 2015, adult food safety and under-poverty adults 3,657 and total $ 6,697.

According to a survey conducted by the Central Statistics Agency, 18.9 percent of the population in Addis Ababa is living below the general poverty line or buying basic food and non-food items.

The food security problem has become a great international agenda, and many countries are addressing the realities of the crisis in various national social services and food security programs. For example, the Hunger Safety Network Program in Kenya, Bossa FAMILY in Brazil, and Project Area Participated in Mexico, etc. The Brazilian Directions and Practices of Practice are presented at the national and city level in order to help us to deal effectively with the good experiences in the country.

CONCEPTUAL FRAME

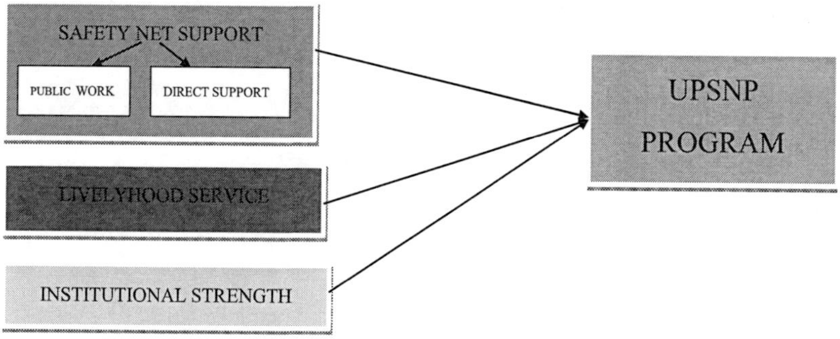

Figure 1. Conceptual Frame

Chapter Three

Research Methodology

3.1 Introduction

For this chapter presents the procedures that were used in conducting this research. It provides an understanding of how the research were conducted and organized in order to obtain the required information. It focuses on research approach, sampling size and sampling technique such as population, sample size, sources of data such as primary and secondary data sources, and data gathering instruments.

3.2 Research Design

The formidable problem that follows the task of defining the research problem is the preparation of the design of the research project, popularly known as the "research design". Decisions regarding what, where, when, how much, by what means concerning an inquiry or a research study constitute a research design. "A research design is the arrangement of conditions for collection and analysis of data in a manner that aims to combine relevance to the research purpose with economy in procedure." In fact, the research design is the conceptual structure within which research is conducted; it constitutes the blue print for the collection, measurement and analysis of data. (Kothary, 2004)

For this study, descriptive type of research design was used. This method had been selected for the reason that it enables the researcher to obtain the information concerning the current status of the occurrence and describe the current status of the title.

3.3 Research Approaches

Basically, the choice of an appropriate research approach depends on the nature of the problem at hand and the type of data needed. To conduct this study, the researcher was use concurrent type of mixed (both qualitative and quantitative) research approaches in order to appropriately address major objectives of the study.

Bryman, (2012), suggested that the combination of both methods emerged as the most valid and reliable way to develop understanding of complex social realities.

3.4 Sampling Size and Sampling Technique

3.4.1 Sampling area

The study has been conducted in Kirkos sub city of Addis Ababa city administration. The reason for selection of the sub city is due to the researcher's familiarity to the study area. Because of the sub city has been the working center of the researcher in the previous years, it has ease of access to reliable information and the prior acquaintance to the area helps to get accurate data from the government officials as well as the sampled households. From the researcher's observation, the urban safety net program is not effectively addressed employment opportunities in the sub city as it fails to create the expected outcomes. To achieve the objective of the research, it was plausible to collect opinion from leaders and civil servants in the woredas and the sub city as well as local community.

Source: Atlas, 2018 Addis Ababa city map.

3.4.2 Sampling Technique

This study was use both probability and non- probability sampling techniques. The target population is the beneficial group of urban safety net program in Kirkos sub city administration. It has 11 woreds as smaller administrative districts and urban productive safety net program in the sub city to conduct first phase 4 woreda and second phase 7 woreda implementation. So this study had been covered 5 woreda to first phase 2 and second phase 3 woreda simple random sampling. As far as probability sampling technique is concerned, the researcher was use simple random sampling technique for the selection of beneficial groups from each woredas. However, non -probability sampling technique, purposive sampling, had been used for the interview of key informants. The researcher believed that the selected key informants could provide enough information concerning the topic under study.

3.4.3 Sampling size

In descriptive studies, one of the procedure had been used and must be carefully planned was the definition of 'population' in which the study to obtain complete and accurate information and refers to the number of populations had been selected from the universe to constitute a sample (Kothari, 2004). Therefore, the researcher was select 10 leaders and civil servants that are directly related with the research and Households using Yamane's (1967) formula.

$$\frac{N}{1+N(e)^2}$$

Where

n = Sample

N = Population Size

e = Margin of error

$$n=\frac{4801}{1+4801\ (.07)^2}=204$$

Based on the above formula the researcher use for the study Target population 4801 and the sample size 204 in numbers.

The size of Target population 4801 Benefiters households

Sample size by household= households

The level of significance= 0.07

3.4.3.1 Sampling Techniques for Qualitative Data Gathering

The Sampling techniques which had been used to select from the target subjects using appropriate techniques as discussed below.

Sampling Technique for Interview: the researcher was making an interview with 10 key informants. Purposive sampling had been used to select. These were leaders of the woreda and Sub city. The reason why these sectors had been select by purposive sampling is to give an opportunity for researcher to select people who can be giving information based on objective set.

3.4.3.2 Sampling Techniques for Quantitative Data Gathering

Simple random sampling has been used to select house hold beneficiaries those who were fill the questionnaires. The researcher prefers to use simple random sampling to select those respondents because it gives equal chance for every independent unit in a population.

3.5 Sources of Data

According to Kotary, 2004, the task of data collection begins after a research problem has been defined and research design/ Plan chalked out while deciding about the method of data collection to be used for the study (Kotary, 2004). So in this study, the researcher was using both primary and secondary sources of data.

3.5.1 The Primary Sources

The primary data are those which are collected afresh and for the first time, and thus happen to be original in character. (Kothari,(2004).

The primary source of this study includes information obtained from the beneficiaries House hold by conducting a semi- structured questionnaire, and in-depth interviews. It included leaders from woreda and sub city.

3.5.2 The Secondary Sources

The secondary data, on the other hand was collect by someone else and which have already been passed through the statistical process (Kothari, (2004).

Secondary source of the study includes review and analysis of documents and reports available in the woreda and sub city. In addition, secondary data were obtain from regulation, proclamation, journals, researches, articles and books had been used to substantiate the information secured the primary data sources.

3.6 Data collection Instruments

3.6.1 Qualitative Data Collection Tools

The qualitative data was gathered through interview and document review.

Interviews: Semi structured interview guide had been used in this research because of flexibility in which new question could be forwarded during interview based on the response of interviewee. This type of interview questioners enabled the respondents to answer the questions in much detail as they want more valid answers about their opinions and values could be obtained and provided an answer about how the respondents contextualize the topic being studied.

Document Review: The document review had been used because it enables the researcher to know much information within short period of time.

3.6.2 Quantitative Data collection Tools

Questionnaires: Since information through other data collection from the majority by other methods is not easily possible then the questionnaire will be used to address the greater number of people in the survey (Dawson, 2002).

Questionnaire provided a more relaxed atmosphere for the respondents to provide their opinion. It had been prepared in both Amharic and English language. Closed ended and open ended types of questionnaires had been develop and used to get focused answers from respondents.

3.7 Data Analyses Method

3.7.1 Qualitative Data Analysis

Qualitative method had been used to analyze and interpret in the form of narration results obtained from the interviews.

3.7.2 Quantitative Data Analysis

The results of this study had been summarized and presented using descriptive statistical tools; Tabulation was used to analyze the quantitative data by using percentage, mean and median.

Chapter Four

Data Presentation, Analysis and Interpretation

4.1 Introduction

This chapter presents results and discusses the sample households Urban Productive Safety Net Program implementation in Kirkose Sub city. Emphasis is given to the targeting process, major challenges and Prospect of the program.

4.1.1. Demographic characteristics

- **Age**

  Table 4.1 shows that the total number of sample households is 199 of which 50.8% is male household heads and the rest 49.2% is female-headed households. With regard to the age of households about 18-45 (59.8%) is in the range of productive age group, 46-64 (33.2%) and 65 + age category accounts for 6.0% alone.

Table 4.1: Age of the sample households

Age	*Frequency*	*Percentage*
<18	2	1.0
18-45	119	59.8
46-64	66	33.2
>65	12	6.0
Total	**199**	100

Source: Household Survey, 2019.

As indicated in the above table, the majority of respondents are within the range of productive age group. Hence, they can actively participate in the public works of PSNP than direct support (except the criteria seated by the PIM in considering health situations of beneficiaries and those who are not able to participate in public work though their age was in production).

- **Martial Status**

Regarding the marital status, 62.3% of the respondents were married, while 23.6% of the respondents unmarried, 0.7% include widowed households and 0.7% respondents are Divorce.

Table 4.2: Marital status of sample households

Marital Status	*Frequency*	*Percentages*
Married	124	62.3%
Unmarried	47	23.6%
Divorced	14	7%
Widowed	14	7%
Total	199	100

Source: Household Survey, 2019.

This table indicated the presence of the targeting of beneficiaries from different groups as supposed to do in PIM (MOARD, 2006). However, this does not mean that there was no problem of targeting, because selection of benificheries constituting different community groups. The main criteria of targeting are poorest of poor. So different groups are not guarantee for the perfection of targeting eligible beneficiaries.

- **Family size**

Table 4.3 shows the family size of the sample households. About 113 (%) households have Three family size or fewer. This is followed by 24.6% households are Four to Six Family and 18.6% seven or more family size.

Table 4.3: Family size of sample households

Family Size	*Frequency*	*Percentage*
1-3	49	24.6
4-6	113	56.8
7+	**37**	**18.6**

Source: Household Survey, 2019.

During the household survey for data collection, the household size of each respondent's HH head members were tried to be included into the data with initial interview. So that the size was tangible and respondents would not deceive. To do this the respondent was asked to list down them by names and any attempts of deceptions was tried to be controlled and minimized as much as possible. The number of family members in the respondent family ranged from 3 to 9. The average family size was 6.

- **Educational Level**

As far as educational level of the sample households concerned Table 4.4 shows that of the 199 households 22 (11.1%) of them have never been to school; 56 (28.1%) can read and write; 54 (27.1%) reached first cycle (1-8); 34 (17.1%) second cycle and 33 (16.6%) above secondary level.

In the above Table, the majority of benificheries indicating read and writes and follow that reached first cycle level of education for the sub city. But in my observation majority of women cannot read and write. This is a good indication of Integrate for education biro plan.

Table 4.4: Educational level

Educational Level	*Frequency*	*Percentage*
Illiterate	22	11.1
Read and write	56	28.1
1-8	54	27.1
9-10	34	17.1
10+	33	16.6
Total	199	100

Source: Household Survey, 2019.

4.2 UPSNP Targeting

Targeting is one of the momentous aspects of social safety net design and implementation. Accordingly, the Program Implementation Manual (PIM) (2004) of Ethiopian PSNP states how to identify the eligible groups/ chronic food insecure household. The mix of community targeting and administrative targeting has been in place. Under this section the practical targeting process, perception of participants of the program with pressures on the process of targeting are discussed.

4.2.1. Urban Productive Safety net Program Targeting Process of Kirkose Subcity

The study area of this research is Kirkose sub city. Kirkose sub city is one of the selected cities among 10 Addis Ababa sub cities under Addis Ababa city Administration. Kirkos sub city covers 11 woredas among these 01,03,07 and 10 woredas are the first round selected woredas and 02,04,05,06,08,09 and 11 woredas are the second phase of urban productive safety net program based on the criteria settled. Urban productive safety net program has three major interrelated sub-programs. These are unconditional direct support, public work sub-program and livelihood sub program. Accordingly, this program is designed and planned to benefit **33,103** beneficiaries. Out of this, **27,508** individuals are screened under public work sub program and the rest **5595** are targeted to assist under unconditional direct support sub-program.

The 1st food security program is started in kirkose sub city May 1/2009 E.C and the 2nd food security program is launched on June /2010 E.C both direct support and Public work sub program in all 11 targeted woredas.

This study focused on first phase 2 sample woreda and second phase 3 sample woreda selected by simple random sampling.

4.2.2 Participation Year of Respondent

In this study sample selection was 5 woreda based on urban safety net implementation. First phase implementation 2 woreda and second implementation 3 woreda proportionally.

Table 4.5: Participation Year

Participation	*Frequency*	*Percentage*
First phase	81	40.7
Second phase	118	59.3

This table indicates that second phase participatory were 59.3% second phase and 40.7% first phase. The result is more focused on the second phase urban productive safety net implementation.

4.2.3 Program component of urban safety net program

Urban productive safety net program are three basic components those are safety net support, livelihood service and institutional strength and financial management. so the first program component safety net support included public work and direct support.

Table 4.6: Program component

Program component	*Frequency*	*Percentage*
Direct Support	59	29.6
Public Work	140	70.4

The study indicates that the sample of 199 beneficiaries direct supports were 29.6% and public work 70.4 %. So it is noted that majority are involved in public works.

4.2.4 Participated Family members

During the 2017 and 2018 program implementation majority 124 (81.9%) of the sample households register for all family members are Included in this program. on other hand 75(37.7%) households all family members are not included in the program.

Table 4.7: Number of Family Members Participated

Family Participation	*Frequency*	*Percentages*
Yes	124	62.3
No	75	37.7
Total	199	100

Source: Household Survey, 2019.

The number of participated family members of the surveyed household among all family participation includes the program.

4.2.3. Perception on the Targeting Process

Under this sub section the beneficiaries view on the targeting process is discussed. City poverty maps are verified by city officials for boundary changes, large movements of people, or changes in the socioeconomic nature of the *woreda* since 2011. Adjustments to boundaries and poverty estimates are made accordingly. The poorest *woredas* (*kebeles* in cities outside of Addis Ababa) are selected for the first year of implementation using 2011 within-city poverty maps. The current population of each *woreda* and the 2011 poverty rate is used to determine the number of target beneficiaries in each *woreda*. In each selected *woreda*, *woreda* officers identify *ketenas* and work with *ketena* and local community leaders from *Ketena* Development Committees, *Iddirs*, women, and youth committees to identify *ketena* boundaries, establish membership of *Ketena* Targeting Committees, and confirm the number of households to be selected from each *ketena*. Lists of registered households and members are updated to take into account any recent changes, and an additional list of unregistered members or households is developed containing those that have been residing in the *woreda* for at least six months. *Woreda* officers and UPSNP staff inform *Ketena* Targeting Committees and the intended beneficiaries (namely, any household resident for at least six months within the *woreda* that is among the poorest in the *ketena*) about the program. *Ketena* Targeting Committees rank and select proposed beneficiaries. Data on households is also collected by the committees and provided to the *woreda* office. The list is made public. The *woreda* office provides information to an independent data collection agency contracted by the project who works with UPSNP staff to sample households for data collection. All non-sampled households that are on the beneficiary list are included in the program. Data is collected and the PMT calculated for sampled households, confirming or querying their assignment to be a beneficiary. Households for whom the assignment to beneficiary or non-beneficiary is queried are discussed by *woreda* officials, program staff, and the *Ketena* Targeting Committee and a final decision is made. The final list of proposed beneficiaries is made public .Selected beneficiaries are informed about the program and asked whether they want to participate. Those eligible for unconditional transfers who would like to receive these transfers register and provide verification of age (being above 65 years) or of their disability or chronic illness that prevents them from being able to perform a co-responsibility for the transfer. Those who are not eligible for the unconditional transfers decide whether they want to participate, given the compensation paid in return for PW, and they register. A *Woreda* Appeals Committee allows targeting decisions to be appealed.

Table 4.8: Targeting of beneficiary

Targeting Selection	*Frequency*	*Percentage*
Targeting Comm.	158	79.4
Woreda Cabinaes	28	14.1
Other	13	6.5
Total	199	100

Source: Household Survey, 2019.

Above table indicate that 28 (14.1%) households reported that the decision made in relation with targeting is by *woreda* cabinets. The other 158 (79.4%) households reported that the selection of beneficiaries is by Targeting committee. Others 13 (6.5 %) they do not know who has to undertake beneficiary households' identification and selection. This simply indicates that the beneficiaries Perception of targeting process.

4.2.4 Targeting Mechanism of Household beneficiary

Table 4.9: Targeting Mechanism

Criteria	*Frequency*	*Percentage*
Poorest of poor	163	81.9
Ownership of asset	9	4.5
No clear criteria	8	4.0
Family size	8	4.0
Political commitment	7	3.5
I don't know	4	2.0
Total	199	100

Source: Household Survey, 2019.

Moreover, in the house holds targeting mechanisms 163 (81.9%) of the 199 reported that generally the poorest of poor are targeted. This is followed by ownership of asset of the household Heads 9 (4.5%) The other 27 (3.5%) households respond that they were selected based on their family size and political commitment for respectively (see Table4.9)

4.2.5 Targeting Fairness

Regarding the targeting fairness 127 (63.8%) of the respondents reported that the process is fair. On the other hand 72 (36.6%) of the sample households reported that the targeting process is unfair.

Table 4.10: Fairness

Fair Targeting	*Frequency*	*Percentage*
Yes	127	63.8
No	72	36.6
Total	199	100

Source: Household Survey, 2019.

Major Achievements and Challenges of Urban Productive Safety Net Program

Performance of the Program

Performance of the program evaluated by the following criteria 160/80.4% of respondents accepts the program planning is participatory and 39/19.6% of the respondents said the program planning is not participatory. From the total 105 /52.8% of respondents said to be the daily transfer payment is not sufficient and only 94/47.2% of respondents agree the daily transfer payment is sufficient. 135/67.2% of respondent accept with public work hour per day is optimum and 64 /32.2% did not accept the public work hours per day is optimum. 94/47.2% of respondents said the budget allocation considers its objective but 105/52.8% of respondents did not agree with the budget allocation. From the total 141/70.9% of respondent said payment are mad at the right time but 58/29.1% of respondents said that transfer payment does not made at the right time.76/38.2% of respondents said the program implementation follows proper monitory and control tools and only 123/61.8% said the implementation does not follow.

Table 4.11: Performance of the program

No	*Statement*	*Response*			
		YES		*No*	
1.	The program planning is participatory	160	80.4	39	19.6
2.	The daily transfer payment is sufficient	94	47.2	105	52.8
3.	Public work hour per day is optimum	135	67.2	64	32.2
4.	Budget allocation consider its objective	94	47.2	105	52.8
5.	Payment are mad at the right time	141	70.9	58	29.1
6.	The program implementation follows proper monitory and control tools	76	38.2	123	61.8

Source: survey 2019.

Achievements of Urban Productive Safety Net Program

To evaluate the achievement of urban productive safety net program based on the following variables. With regard to Income Level only 77% of respondents have said high improvement. Food consumption expenditure, 73% of respondents highly agree but 75% have said medium change in food consumption expenditure in case of saving 81% of respondents have said highly improvement. 72% of respondents said urban productive safety net program improve Social participation. 69% of respondents said the program highly improve Employment creation. 60% of respondents said high improvement in Green area development. From the total respondent 64% agree to urban productive safety net program reduce vulnerability of participant.

Table 4.12: Achievements of urban productive safety net program

No	Statement	*Response*			
		Very high	*High*	*Medium*	*Low*
1.	Income Level	40	77	60	22
2.	Food Consumption	30	73	75	21
3.	Saving	66	81	44	8
4.	Social participation	61	12	48	18
5.	Employments creation	47	69	57	26
6.	Green area	60	57	59	23
7.	Reducing Vulnerability	45	53	64	37

Source: survey 2019.

Success of the Program

As indicated below Table 4.12, 69.8% of respondents said that urban productive safety net program succeeds its goal. 30.2% of respondents said that the program did not succeed its goal. The reason is that, they do have not enough medical treatment and work time is not appropriate to engage additional work.

Additionally, the interview conducted with the success of urban productive safety net program showed that the program encourages in saving culture and additional work to avoid help others.

Table 4.13: Program Success

Statement	*Response*			
	Yes		*No*	
Programe Succeed	139	69.8	60	30.2

Source: survey 2019.

Major Strengths of the Urban Productive Safety Net Program in Addressing Food Insecurity Problem of the Sub-City Poor

Urban productive safety net program has a recent practice in Addis Ababa city and also in Kirkos sub city. After two years the program has its own strength in reducing food insecurity problem of the participant's households. According to the findings of the study (questionnaire and interview results), the major strengths of urban productive safety net program are the following:

> The Program has changed attitude in work culture and saving is more sustainable of benificheries. It indicates that to get any of payment or decrease in food consumption to save it. Most of the participants have improved social interaction between them. Most of subcity area to be clean and attractive by Green area.

Major Challenges of the Program during Implementation

Urban productive safety net program faces many challenges. As per the respondents response the program face some limitation:

> The major problem with targeting process is less consideration of the aged and disabled Some households have dependency attitude to stay in the program. The current payment for public work is lower as compared with increasing food prices. Safety material and logistics was not purchase timely. There was lack of medical treatments for participant who cause illness at the public work. There was lack of adequate trainings about the program for household who participant in the program. Additionally Interview In woreda cabinets and officer Time tightness of for life skill training, Lack of awareness

at community level and attitude of dependency among public workable bodies, Dalliance of collected solid wastes at proper disposal cities, Lack of coordination among key stakeholders such as MCC, TCC and Councils, Problem of movement direct support beneficiaries in opening bank account, Lack of full awareness and training for stakeholder & *woreda* officials, The shortage of logistic & office equipment ,There was lack of adequate transport for officers which have support and monitor the program implementations.

Chapter Five

Summary, Conclusions and Recommendations

5.1 Summary of Major Findings

In this study, an attempt was made to examine the benefits derived from and the challenges encountered in implementation of urban productive safety net program particularly in Kirkose Sub city of Addis Ababa.

The objective of the program is creating job opportunities for citizens under poverty line in their local areas to improve their living standard and finally avoid poverty.

The study made use of mixed (both quantitative and qualitative) approach with descriptive method. Data was collected through questionnaires and interview. The study tries to examine the challenges, prospect and Targeting process of the benificheries of urban productive safety net program. The major findings of the study are summarized as follow:

The beneficiaries target and selection for program implementation is positively perceived by program participant. But beneficiary identification and selection in the first phase of the program implementation suffered from corruption by the targeting committee. In addition, from the second phase implementation community some sort of segregation by tribe during the vote for PSNP was observed. In line with this still no measure of participants has been taken, and attempt of reducing relativism among the communities using strong local mechanisms have had little impact during the targeting process.

Majority of the performance of the program are improvement on program planning is participatory, public work hour per day is optimum, payment made at the right time. But with regard to the daily transfer payment, budget allocation the performance of the program is lower than the projected and the program implementation less follows proper monitory and control tools.

Majority 69.8% of the respondent agrees with the program success. 30.2% of the respondent have not sure whether the program succeed its goal or not. According to the respondent the reason is that, to have less monitoring and control system, payment is not sufficient, the program (public work) expose to heath problem, the transfer payment did not sell enough food, and the work time is not appropriate for the benefits to engage in additional work.

The programs have its own strength in reducing food insecurity problem. According to the findings of the study (questionnaire and interview results), the major strengths of urban productive safety net program are changing saving culture, social participations are increase and increase income level of households. It increase food availability for very poor participant, Women headed household became temporary job owner as a result improve purchasing power of poor household and developing work culture.

Urban productive safety net program faces many challenges. Some of those are benefiters target and selection was sometimes errors were observed. There was lack of adequate trainings about the main objective of the program for households as a result some households have dependency attitude to stay in the program.

The current payment for public work is lower as compared with increasing food prices. Safety material and logistics was not purchase timely as a result illness at the public work increases with lack of medical treatments for participant. Some of the benefiter faces delay in transfer payment as a result the benefiters could not meet their daily demand. The working time is not suitable for participant to engage in additional work.

The communities who have non-participant are not protecting infrastructures made by safety net program as a result some infrastructures (green and beauty area) damage by persons who live in that community. Sometimes delay in transfer payment. There where lack of adequate transport for officers who have support and monitor the program.

Finally, lack of sectorial coordination among sectors like Micro and small enterprise office, Labor and Social affair office, Women and Children affair office, Youth and Sport office solid west collection and disposal office and other to support public work made by urban productive safety net program.

5.2 Conclusion.

The implementation of urban productive safety net program in kirkose sub city has caused significant benefits in most part of its operation, yet different factors challenge the program. In general, the following conclusion was drowning from the findings and summary of the study.

There is improvement on income earning and spent for food consumption, saving culture, awareness on environmental protection and social connection.

According to the finding of the study, the following are major challenges of productive safety net program in implementation. The current payment for public work is lower as compared with increasing food prices because of this; same households have no change in food consumption level. Safety material and logistics was not purchase timely as a result illness at the public work increases with lack of medical treatments for participant.

There was lack of adequate trainings about the main objective of the program for households as a result some households have dependency attitude to stay in the program. The communities who have non-participant are not protecting infrastructures made by safety net program as a result some infrastructures (green and beauty area) damage by persons who live in that community. There where lack of adequate transport for officers who have support and monitor the program. Finally, lacks of sectorial coordination among sectors that support public work made by UPSNP as a result it affect the successes of the program.

5.3 Recommendations

Based on the finding the following recommendations were forwarded for the benefiter's households and kirkose sub city administration.

Targeting

- Successful Targeting process and citizen engagement activities are improved.
- During the retargeting process local mechanisms to avoid bias towards relatives must be strengthened. For instance, the problem of voting for the same tribe among the community must be discouraged, and the essence of good governance should be

penetrated to the community level to deny the corruptive activities at the woreda and ketena level during the retargeting process.

- Creating full awareness for stakeholders, partners, Woreda executives, ketena targeting and appeal committees and program beneficiaries.

Challenges

- The current increasing food prices, heavy reliance on cash economy, high transaction costs, high housing cost and rents have to be need revised in payment for both public work and direct support.
- Fulfilling human and material resources before program implementation was essential.
- The sub-city administration has to give support on medical treatment for participants who cause illness at the public work.
- The sub-city administration should be facilitating adequate transport for officers who monitor, technically support, and evaluate public work activities.
- Strong sectorial coordination ought to be created among sectors like Micro and small enterprise office, Labor and Social affair office, Women and Children affair office, Youth and Sport office, Solid waste collection and disposal office and other to support urban productive safety net program.
- Identification of potential areas of public work activities at Woreda level with communities participation.

Reference

Addis Ababa City Administration Micro and Small Enterprises Development Bureau Job creation and food security Agency Structural organization 2009 Addis Ababa.

Addis Ababa City Administration Micro and Small Enterprises Development Bureau Job creation and food security agency Council Organization and Proposed Draft Instructions 80/2009.

Agrekon, J. (2009). The Status of Household Food Security Targets In South Africa Available at https://core.ac.uk/download/pdf/6678974.pdf on 7th Feb., 2019.

Bryman, A. (2012). Social Research Methods.4th ed., Oxford University Publisher, New York.

Dagnew Eshete (1994). Food Security, Household Coping Strategies With Food Shortages And Food Security Planning *Approaches.* Prepared For SCF-UK Sponsored Training/Workshop Participants of SERP Staff, Held at Jijiga.

Dawson, C. (2002). Practical Research Method: A User –Friendly Guide to Mastering Research. How to Books Ltd, United Kingdom.

De Cristofaro, C., and Collins, S. (2010).A literature review. *AANA Journal, 78*(6). Retrieved from www.aana.com. Used by permission. Writing Center from Key, K.L.

Devereux. S and Wheele. R. (2004). ETHIOPIA'S Productive Safety Net Programme Centre for Social Protection, Institute of Development Studies.

Federal Democratic Republic of Ethiopia Urban food security strategy (Council approved by the Council of Ministers in April 2007, Addis Ababa).

Frigenti, L., and A. Harth, (1998). The Growth of Social Funds and Public Works and Employment Projects in Sub-Saharan Africa, Water and Urban 2 and Institutional and Social Policy Divisions, Africa Region, World Bank, Washington, D.C.

FAO, (2004). Food Insecurity and Vulnerability in Nepal: Profiles of Seven Vulnerable groups Food Security and Agricultural Projects Analysis

Service (ESAF) ESA Working Paper No.04-10.UN Available to http://www.mountainforum.org/sites/default/files/pub/1406.pdf.

Girma B. and Holden Stein. The Impact of Ethiopia's Productive Safety Net Program (PSNP) on Fertilizer Adoption by Smallholder Farmers: Evidence from Tigray, Northern Ethiopia Norwegian University of Life Sciences.

Getachew Diriba, (1995). Economy at the cross road: Famine and food insecurity in Ethiopia, A.A: Care International Ethiopia.

Ghattas, H. (2014). Food Security and Nutrition in the Context of the Nutrition Transition.TechnicalPaper.FAO, Rom.

Guush. B, Kumar. J, Alemayehu. S (2011) The impact of Ethiopia's Productive Safety Nets and Household Asset Building Programme, International Food Policy Research Institute December 30, 2011 Address for correspondence: Dr. John Hoddinott, International Food Policy Research Institute, 2033 K Street NW, Washington DC 20006 USA.

Holzman, R., Jorgensen. S. (2000). "Social Risk management: A new conceptual frame work for Social protection and beyond", World Bank, Social protection discussion paper No.9904.Washington DC, USA

Kothari C. (2004) Research Methodology: Methods and Techniques: 2nd Ed. New Delhi: New Age International Publisher.

Lal, R et al 2002. Food Security and Environmental Quality in Developing World. USA: Lewis Publisher.

Maxwell, S. (2001). Food Security in Developing Countries: Issues and Options for the 1990s1.

Ministry of Agriculture and Rural Development (MOARD) 2006 *Productive Safety Net Program: Program Implementation Manual* (rev.). Addis Ababa, Ethiopia.

MOA, (Ministry of Agriculture) 2014. Productive Safety Net Program Phase IV, Program Implementation.

Ministry of Urban Development and Housing Federal urban job creation and food security agency (FUJCFSA) Urban productive safety net program, *public work Gide line* January, 2017 Addis Ababa

Nayyar (2002). Impact of Productive Safety Net Program in Ethiopia .Available At www.Rff.Org/Files/Sharepoint/Workimages/.../Efd-DP-09-05.Pdf; Accessed on 7th Feb., 2019.

Reutlinger, S. (1998). Poverty and Hunger: Issues and Options for Food Security in Developing Countries.

Urban Productive Safety Net Program Implementation Manual, by Ministry of urban development and Housing (MOUDH), 2016.

World Bank, 1986.Poverty and Hunger: Issues and Options for Food Security III Developing Countries. The World Bank: Washington.

World Bank, 2010.Ethiopia's Productive Safety Net Program (PSNP) Nitrating Disaster and Climate Risk Management

World Bank, 2015, HABITAT III New Urban Agenda, Draft outcome document for adaptation in Quito, October 2016 (Sep 2016) Safety-Nets & Social Protection Unit Program and Policy Division socialprotection@wfp.org

World Food Program, (1996).Productive Safety Net Program **(PSNP)**

World Food Program, 2012. National Food Security and Nutrition Strategy

Abbrevations

ADLI : Agricultural Development Led Industrialization
CAS : Country Assistance Strategy
CIDA : Canadian International development Agency
CSA : Central Statistics Authorities
DFID : Department for International Development
ECA : Economic Commission for Africa
FAO : Food and Agriculture organization
FDRE : Federal Democratic Republic of Ethiopia
FSS : Food Security Strategy
GOE : Government of Ethiopia
GTP : Great Transformation Plane
MOUDH : Ministry of Urban Development and Housing
NNP : National Nutrition Program
OFSP : Other Food Security Program
DPs : Development Partners
PDO : Program Development Objectives
PSNP : Productive Safety Net Program
PW : Public Work,
SDGs : Sustainable Development Goals
UFSS : Urban Food Security Strategy
ULGs : Urban Local Governments
ULGDP : Urban Local Government Development Project
UJCFSP : Urban Job Creation and Food Security Program
UPSNP : Urban Productive Safety Net Program
USAID : United States Agency for International Development

Index